Squiggles:
So much writing
So much fun
So much creativity

Patricia Pavelka, author
Lois Schenking, editor

The Cardinal

How beautifully the cardinal does fly
As it travels up, frighteningly high
Thanks to its uplifting wings
Which are wondrous things
The cardinal can reach its home in the sky

A cardinal's feathers are crimson and bright
Even in the dimmest skis of the night
Although its tiny beak
May make it seem quite weak
The cardinal is a marvelous sight

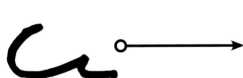

Husky Trail Press LLC
PO Box 705
East Lyme, CT 06333

www.huskytrailpress.com

The philosophy of Husky Trail Press is based on the courage, leadership, and loyalty of the Husky. The Husky's ability to always do its very best and excel, no matter how difficult the obstacles on the trail, is an encouragement to us all.

Husky Trail Press LLC
PO Box 705
East Lyme, CT 06333
860-739-7644
888-775-5211
860-691-8066 fax
www.huskytrailpress.com

Editor: Lois Schenking

ISBN No. 978-0-9722918-5-9

Table of Contents

Introduction 5

How To Use This Book 5

Part I...7

Use squiggles as prompts for quick writes 8

Coordinate the squiggle activity with your content area 10

Use squiggles to help students recognize and spell sight words 11

Use squiggles for descriptions 12

Use squiggles as prompts for stories 14

Coordinate the squiggle with your basal stories and/or novels 16

Coordinate the squiggle with your math curriculum 19

Turn your squiggle into a _____ 20

Coordinate the squiggle with different poetry forms 21

Practice skills with squiggle pictures 25

Make connections to your life with squiggles 27

Part II 29

Squiggle Reproduciles 30

Student Writing Forms 51

Introduction

What are squiggles?
Squiggles are quick designs made on pieces of paper. Students take their squiggles, turn them into pictures, and then write about them.

Who uses squiggles?
Squiggles can be used with kindergarteners through middle school students. They can be used with any level of ability.

Where do squiggles fit into our daily routines?
Squiggles can be used in a writing center or as an activity during independent work.

Why squiggles?
The use of squiggles is a great way to get students to write.

When do students work on squiggles?
Students can work on squiggles during assignment times. Squiggles are also a great management tool for, "I'm done, now what do I do?" The students have pocket folders at their desks where they keep a squiggle picture and writing. Throughout the day, after students have completed assigned tasks, they take out their folders and continue to work on their pictures and writing.

How do squiggles fit into our curriculum?
Squiggles can be used in any curriculum area. Students can turn their squiggles into things they have learned about in science or social studies and then write about them. They can turn their squiggles into something that happened in a book and write about it. They can turn their squiggles into pictures of word problems they have created. The list is endless!

How To Use This Book

Part I:
    Above red line: squiggle ideas, extensions, and the actual squiggle used.
    Below red line: students' samples.

Part II:
    Twenty-one reproducible squiggles.
    Four reproducible writing forms.

Part I

Ideas
Extensions
Actual Squiggle Used
Students' Samples

Use squiggles as prompts for quick writes.

Students can turn their squiggles into anything they want and then write about them. Notice the form on the four samples below: the squiggle is on top and writing is on the bottom of the paper. These are samples where the teacher has used the form found on page 51. Students do not see a whole piece of lined paper and get overwhelmed by the amount of writing they think they must complete. Students may ask, "How long does it have to be?" The answer is, "Try to fill all of the lines." Each week just change the squiggle on the top of the paper and you have a new writing activity.

What did students turn their squiggle into?

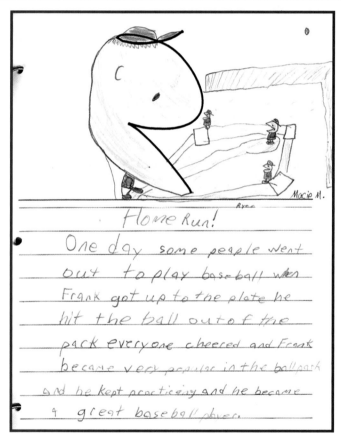

a baseball player

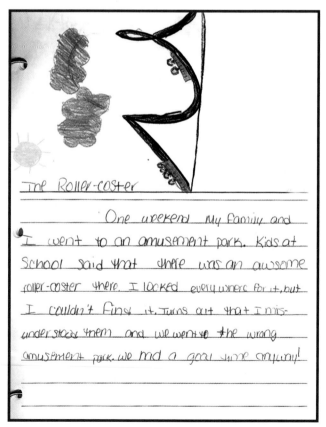

a roller coaster

quick writes (cont.)

The Christmas Story!
A true Story!
Mayrie M.

One day on Dec. 23 my church had a christmas program. So they ask me what did I want to be I said "an angel". And then we had to make the castuem so I would look like an angel. It was hard work and on Dec. 25 we did our program. They said that we did very good.

The End

a self-portrait

One day me and my friends were going to go walking on this road, but it started raining so we couldn't. Me and my friends didn't know what to do so we stayed inside and put a movie in and as soon as the movie got done rewinding it stopped raining. So we went back outside and road my go cart. And thats the way our day went.

a snake

Coordinate the squiggle activity with your content area.

Students need to turn their squiggles into something they have learned in science and/or social studies and then write mini-reports. Some topics that have been used for squiggles are: transportation, the ocean, states, community helpers, things that magnets attract, three states of matter, the farm, plants, and mammals. The list is endless. This is a great way to get expository writing into the curriculum. Later, students can use the squiggles for reviewing what they have learned during their science and/or social studies time. Below are examples from a unit on Native Americans. The picture on the bottom shows how squiggle projects can be used for a bulletin board display.

Use squiggles to help students recognize and spell sight words.

Give students a prompt to use with their pictures. The prompt is a sentence that contains high frequency words. It should be no longer than four words. Below are samples using the prompt, "This is a _____."

This is a DUCK
Hayley

This is a vine.
BAILS

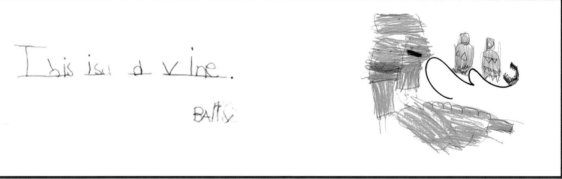

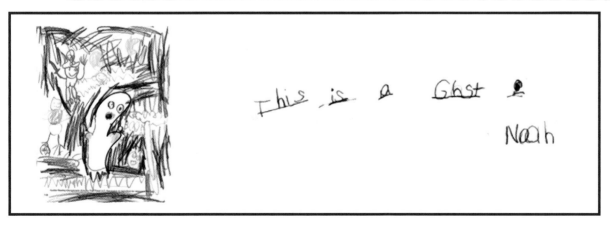

This is a Ghst
Naoh

Use squiggles for descriptions.

Some students panic when asked to write a story. Squiggles are great for students to use when writing a description about what they have drawn. Tell them not to worry about characters, plot, actions, etc. They just look at their pictures and write what they see. Soon, very reluctant writers become more confident writers when squiggles are used this way.

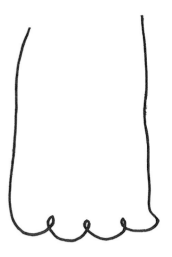

descriptions (cont.)

This is me outside in sun next to the trees and the flower

I like my Shrt.
I like my eyes becaus it is blue.
I like my hire becua it is yellow.

Use squiggles as prompts for stories.

Students can turn their squiggles into anything they want and then write stories about them.

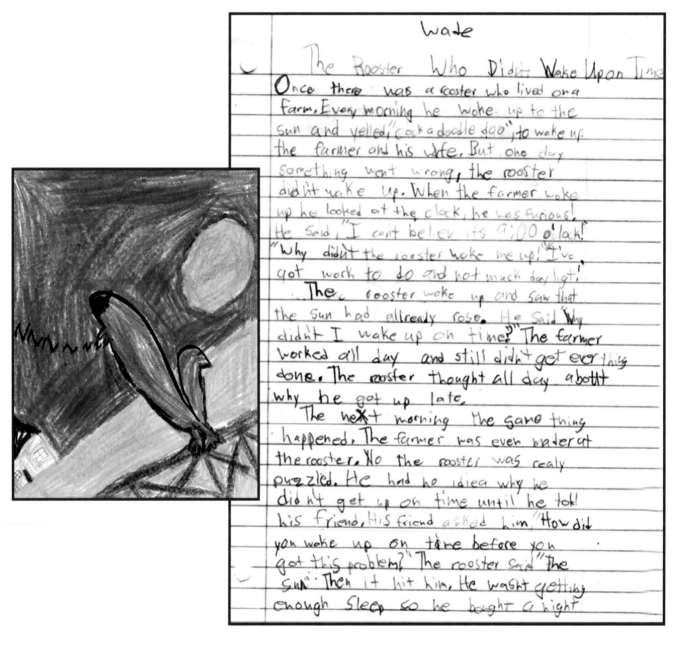

Wate

The Rooster Who Didn't Wake Upon Time

Once there was a rooster who lived on a farm. Every morning he woke up to the sun and yelled "cockadoodle doo" to wake up the farmer and his wife. But one day something went wrong, the rooster didn't wake up. When the farmer woke up he looked at the clock, he was furious! He said, "I can't believ its 9:00 o'clock! "Why didn't the rooster wake me up! "I've got work to do and not much day ligt!"

The rooster woke up and saw that the sun had allready rose. He said "Why didn't I wake up on time?" The farmer worked all day and still didn't get everthing done. The rooster thought all day aboutt why he got up late.

The next morning the same thing happened. The farmer was even mader at the rooster. No the rooster was realy puzzled. He had no idiea why he didn't get up on time until he told his friend. His friend asked him, "How did you wake up on time before you got this problem?" The rooster said "The sun". Then it hit him. He wasnt getting enough sleep so he bought a light

Once there was a momma fish and baby fish. They both lived in the ocean. They had lots of friends. and where very whithy too. But One day the baby fish was play with his momma and a net came down and picked the momma fish and the bady up and start taking them to the shallw end of the ocean. They trid to git out of the net by swimming forwad the bottem of the ocean. But the momma fish said wait lets try to bit the net and the net brook in half and the momma fish and the baby fish was Free and the fish lived happily ever ater.

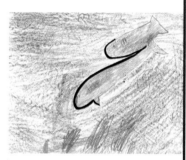

My name is Sorrel. I am a dragon how spits blue Fire. My best Friend is a red dragon named Coral. Coral and I went on a trip to america. Our First stop was New York. Sence were girls were going to go shopping. After we went shopping we went home.

Coordinate the squiggle with your basal stories and/or novels.

Students need to turn the squiggles into something that refers to a story or novel. Topics that may be used are: characters, setting, problem/solution, cause/effect, favorite part, theme, etc. The examples below are from the story, "*The Fury of a Hurricane*," found in an anthology. The examples on the next page are from the novel *The Indian In the Cupboard*. The examples on page 18 are from *The Gingerbread Boy* and *A Hundred and One Dalmations*.

Darryl

In the story The Fury of a Hurricane it said that people got down on there knees and prayed that the winds would slow and go away from there City.

Cecilia

On this picture I drew water trees and clouds. their showing how it would be like if a hurricane hits your city its showing waves that are going crazy and trees that are knocked down. Also I feel sorry for Florida that had to survive the hurricane and some didn't survive and some lost their homes and this is a picture of how Florida was when the hurrican past through there.

That day when Omri's brother thought he was a crook cause his football shorts were missing. And when he went to school with the Indian Little Bear and Cowboy Boone. Also his principle got sick cause of him and the store man thought he was a crook. When he got home his brother had got so mad he hid the cupboard. Now Omri found his brothers shorts and told Omri that his cupboard was in the attick

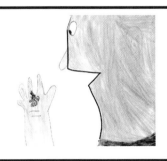

Omri's birthday is here. His best friend Patrick got him a little toy indian, it was plastic. Omri put the indian into cupboard and went to sleep when he woke up the indian was a real person but the size of a toy.

Omri got a cupboard for his birthday. The cupboard didn't have a key. Omri found a key that fit. The key was his great-grandmother's. The key and the cupboard turned a plastic indian to life.

Can't catch me I'm the gingerbread boy. Then he met A cow and the cow chased the gingerbread boy. The little old women, and The little old man chased after the cow.

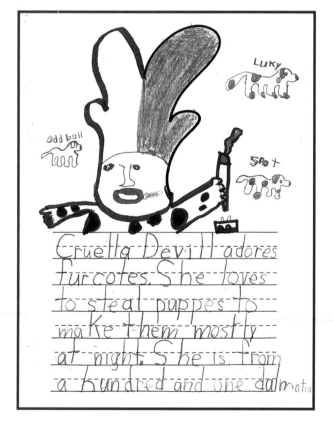

Cruella Devill adores furcotes. She loves to steal puppes to make them mostly at night. She is from a hundred and one dalmatia

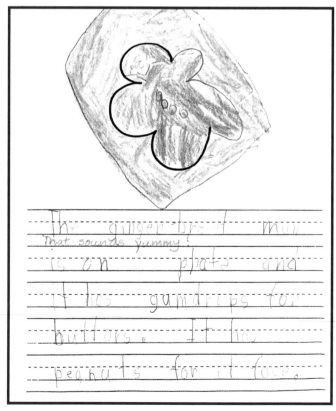

The gingerbread man That sounds yummy! is on plate and It has gumdrops for buttons. It has peanuts for it face.

Coordinate the squiggle with your math curriculum.

The example below shows how to use a squiggle picture to practice writing and solving word problems.

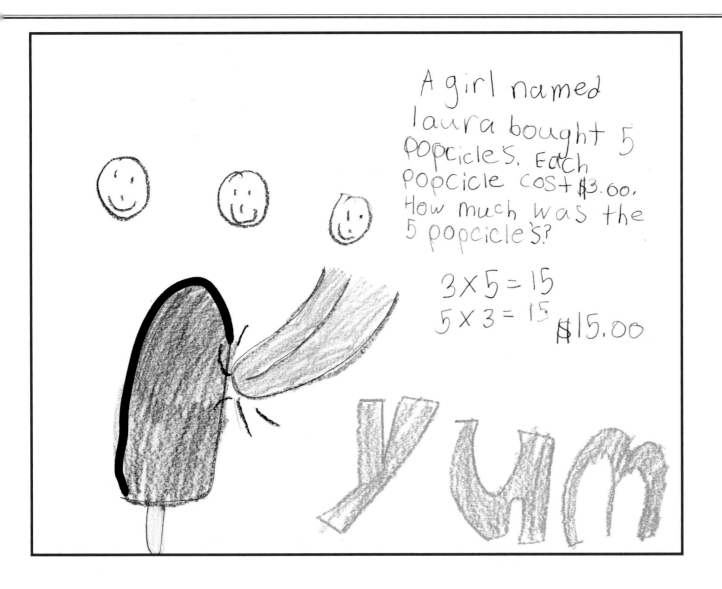

A girl named laura bought 5 popcicles. Each popcicle cost $3.00. How much was the 5 popcicles?

$3 \times 5 = 15$
$5 \times 3 = 15$ $15.00

yum

Turn your squiggle into a _____.

Give students a specific object to create with their squiggles and then write about them. The examples below show students who turned their squiggles into hats.

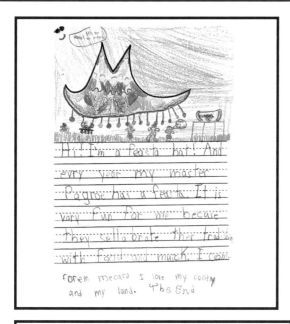

Hi! I'm a feasta hat! And evry year my master Pagroe has a feasta. It is vary fun for me because they cellabrate ther tradi with food and musck. I com forem mecaco I love my contry and my land. The End

Hay I'm lala and I leve in Mexico. They col me lala Becaus I olwais laik to sing the so lalala.

My first silly hat I got today. My hourse likes it. So I bot it and now I wair it. I love my hat. I will never sell my hat.

Bye—Bye

Coordinate the squiggle with different poetry forms.

After turning squiggles into pictures, students can write poems about them. Poetry forms they can use include: haiku, limerick, free verse, cinquain, etc.

Catch of the Day

The penguin may seem like a cuddly bird
With its body painted black and white
But when it comes to hunting for food
He will put up quite a fight.

He scans the Arctic Ocean
And spies a helpless fish
The fish is completely unaware
He will be the penguin's side dish.

The penguin plunges into the water
He can paddle very deep
The chances of this fish surviving
Are becoming extremely steep.

The penguin swims, fish clenched in his beak
His family is waiting by the shore
He quickly dispenses the food to his kids
And after goes hunting for more.

His family feasts upon his catch
It's been the only meal of the day
But all their hopes come soaring back
Once again, Father sees more prey.

The Cardinal

How beautifully the cardinal does fly
As it travels up, frighteningly high
Thanks to its uplifting wings
Which are wondrous things
The cardinal can reach its home in the sky

A cardinal's feathers are crimson and bright
Even in the dimmest skis of the night
Although its tiny beak
May make it seem quite weak
The cardinal is a marvelous sight

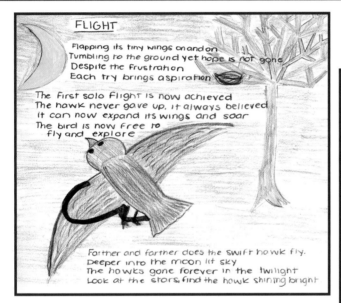

FLIGHT

Flapping its tiny wings on and on
Tumbling to the ground yet hope is not gone
Despite the frustration
Each try brings aspiration

The first solo flight is now achieved
The hawk never gave up, it always believed
It can now expand its wings and soar
The bird is now free to
fly and explore

Farther and farther does the swift hawk fly.
Deeper into the moon lit sky
The hawks gone forever in the twilight
Look at the stars, find the hawk shining bright

Eyes of pure gold,
Yet bitter and cold

Talons of stone,
Chilled through the bone

Never getting old,
Only more bold

Always alone,
Yet no sigh or moan

Alone the owl is born,
And alone it will die,
With no heart to be torn,
Just the freedom to fly

poetry forms (cont.)

These examples integrate the science topic "Cicadas" with the language arts topic "Poetry." An example of student assessment is below on the lower right.

Deep beneath the ground, cicadas eat for 17 years
when the ground temp is just right, cicadas emerge with their peers
Roots keep them fed, while living underground
On trees and sidewalks are where they can be found
leaving their exoskeletons clinging from trees
Dont worry, cicadas dont sting like bees
You'll also see their trillions of holes
Instead they only leave your trees partially whole
Whatever, don't stare into their red beady eyes
When eating them never eat their wings or you just might die
The cicadas are infamous for hypnotizing you
The damage from the cicadas might make you buy many things new
Cover your ears because they make a deafening sound as they fly by
The cicadas will then die and you will see them fall by
Dont worry, cicadas won't eat your lunch
When the cicadas are all dead you won't be able to walk
with out making a crunch.
Watch out when they fly by, they just might stick on you like glue
When they are all gone there is no reason to feel blue

Cicada Poem Critique
18 lines ___ ✓
6 Facts:
1. Spend 17 years underground
2. Drink sap from Tree roots
3. Dig tunnels to get to the surface
4. Male cicadas make noise to find Females
5. Cicadas aren't harmful to humans
6. We can eat them
Rhyme Scheme: aabbccddee ffgghhiijj

Jennifer follows the poem's criteria very well. Her poem is 20 lines long, which is two more than the minimum of 18. She also has six facts about cicadas. For example, the poem says that cicadas drink sap from tree roots when they are underground. Jennifer has a very obvious rhyme scheme of aabbccddeeffgghhiijj. Some of the rhyming words are underground, sound, liquid, bid and not/pot.

CICADAS

Out of holes in the ground they climb,
Each hole no bigger than a dime.
Up the near-by trees do they clamber,
Perched with their saw-like limbs of amber.
High up among the leafy limbs,
They try to sing their loving hymns.
You'd think they would have something to say,
The way they keep on tuning to play.
Their off-key chorus forever in my ears,
Just wishing it was the music of the spheres.
Crunchy, crusty, clinging in many clusters,
Exoskeletons retaining a strange lustre.
Each about a metric inch long,
Some say they look ugly and wrong.
You'd think they would hurry up and leave.
What do they have to really achieve?
Listen now and you will surely hear,
Their piercing melody, it's crystal clear.

Cicadas arrived like jets in flight
They infiltrated our area just overnight.
Before they surfaced, they lived underground
It was hard to imagine what life would be like with them around
For 17 years, they waited to emerge from the earth
Like a baby being born, waiting for the birth
Cicadas fly in packs, searching for the perfect mate
Like human beings looking for a date.
They chatter and fly and feed on trees,
Smaller then birds but bigger than bees.
Some people are imaginative in their use of cicadas,
Frying, dipping in chocolate or putting in fahitas!
People that live in older areas of the state will have more cicadas around
Others that live in new areas will have less because of the disturbance of the ground.
Cicadas are like pesky neighbors and can get under your skin
Good thing their stay is temporary and they are not permanent pets or kin.
Over the last few days, a million cicadas I have heard and seen,
I am very willing to wait for them again in another seventeen!

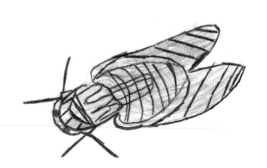

Practice skills with squiggle pictures.

After creating pictures, students can practice using specific writing/language arts skills in their writing. For example: quotation marks, commas in a series, or different kinds of ending punctuation may be chosen. Below is an example of creating a squiggle picture as a prompt for writing about three kinds of ending marks of punctuation.

This is a tree I found in my back yard.
This tree is taller then my House!
Have you seen a tree taller than your house?

practice skills (cont.)

After creating two pictures from the same squiggle, students can write
dialogue between two things in their pictures.

Make connections to your life with squiggles.

Students turn their squiggles into something about their lives and then write about it. In the examples below, students wrote about a vacation, the family pet, and taking the bus to school.

Once upon a time me, my dad and my mom and my brother all want to green bay, to go see the packers play.

This is my dog Sandy. She is in my backyard. It is lunch time. It is time to eat.

I ride the bus to school. The bus is vary big. The bus has a lot of rizes. The bus is going to Ladd. The bus is one bus of my school.
Ashley

connections (cont.)

ERICA

Toni and I went da wo
The Stars and we was lasing
to most it. Then my sister
called a WC The Stars and she was
lasing to most it to.

Tiffany,
This is a hert that
you love somone with
like I love my broth
because the makes me laf I
Love every one in The Hoiwude

Part II

Squiggle Reproducibles
Student Writing Forms

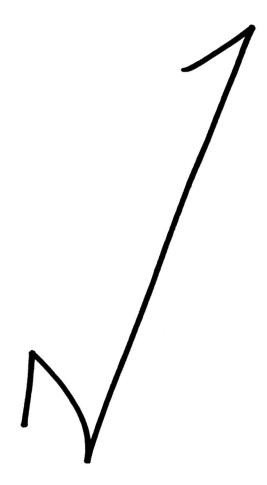

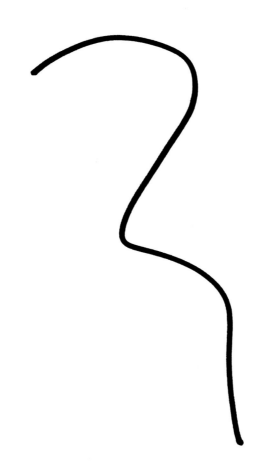

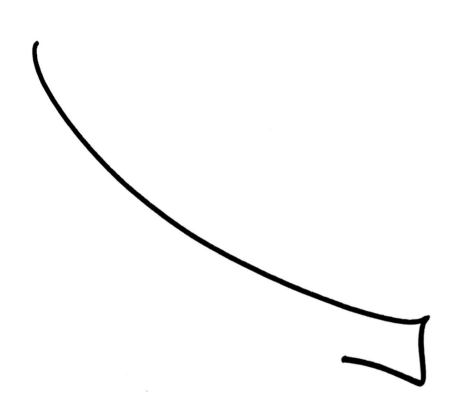

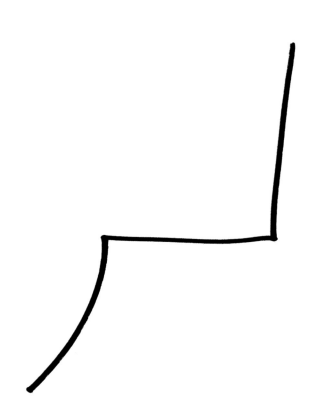

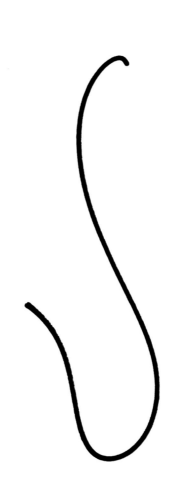

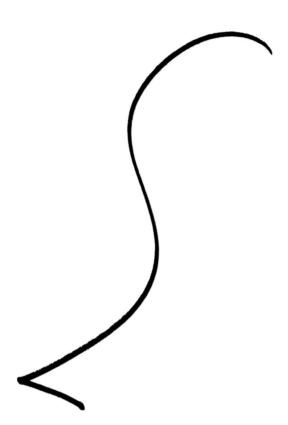

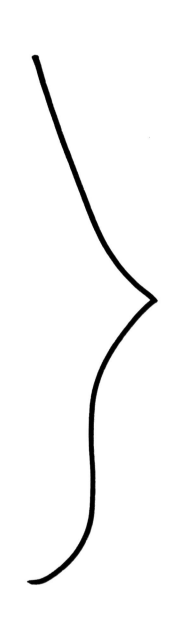

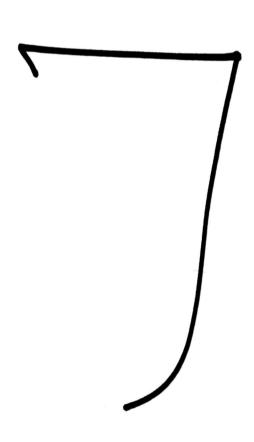

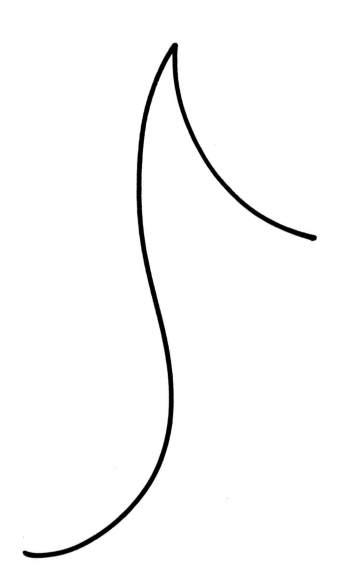

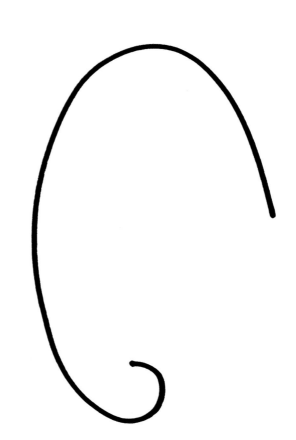

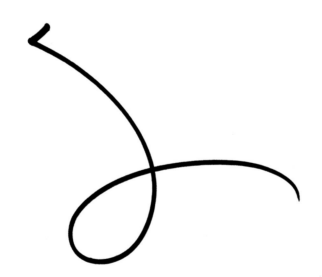

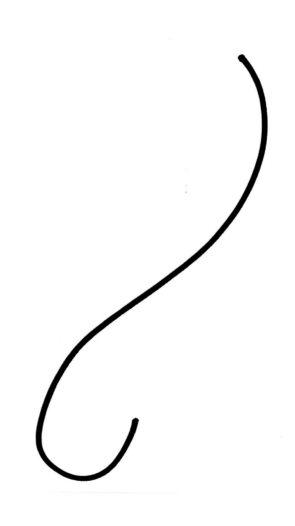

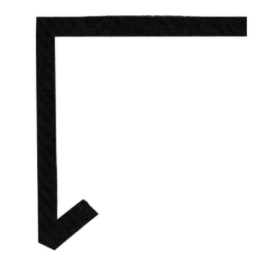

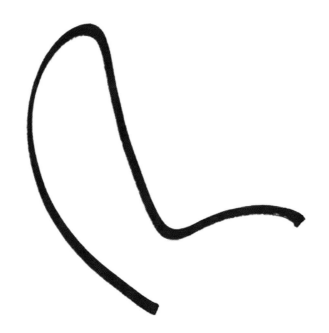

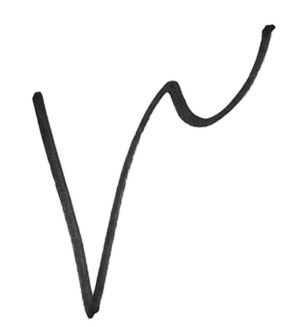

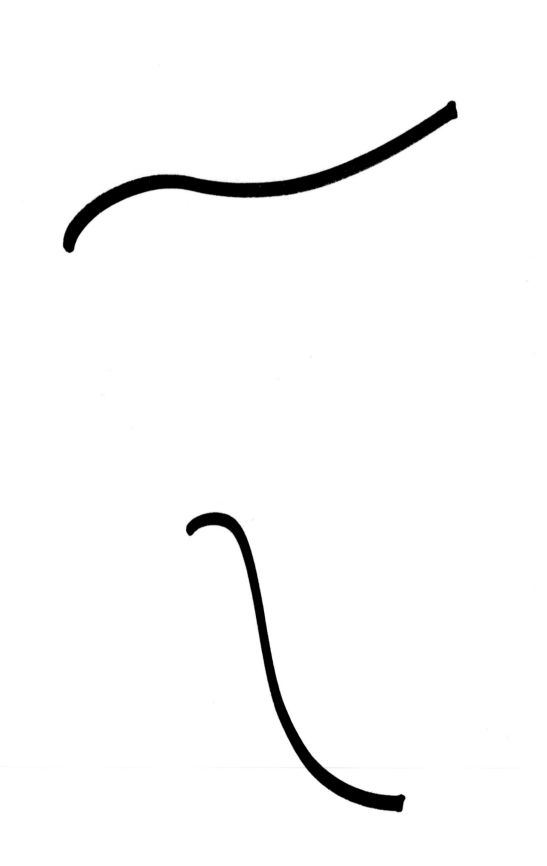

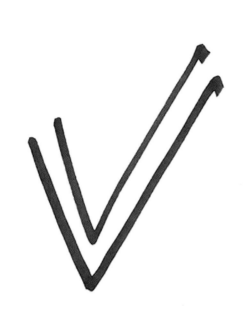

cut here

cut here

cut here

cut here

Books Authored by Pat Pavelka

Cubes
Discussion Activities for Literacy and Skill Development
Teachers will liven up whole group discussions, mini-lessons, and small group interactions. Students will apply and utilize skills, not just memorize! Grades 1-8.

Differentiated Assignments
This book demonstrates how to differentiate the daily assignments teachers give students. Teachers plan one activity that can be completed by students of different ability levels. Grades 1-8. Flip tab.

Guided Reading Management
Structure and Organization for the Classroom
This book is a comprehensive manual showing educators how to structure and manage their guided reading programs. Grades 1-3. 158 pages.

Create Independent Learners
Teacher-Tested Strategies for All Ability Levels
This book is full of ideas, strategies, and activities to help all ability-level students become independent learners. Grades 1-5. 160 pages.

Making the Connection
Learning Skills Through Literature
Pat demonstrates how to move toward creating a literature-based reading program that actively involves students in learning. One book is for grades K-2 (136 pages) and one book is for grades 3-6 (144 pages).

Foodle
Foodle is a fascinating fish with an "interesting" attribute. He is also a little uncertain of the deep, dark, mysterious ocean where he lives. One day he comes face-to-face with a gigantic baleen whale... Children's book. 32 color pages. Educational activities included.

The Adventures of Victor
Victor the Cat loved his life and friends in the city. One day his family moved to the country. The sounds, smells, and animals were as strange to Victor as he was to them. Then an incident happens... Children's book. 32 color pages. Educational activities included.

Narration and Songs from *The Adventures of Victor*
CD and Cassette.

www.huskytrailpress.com